Bones of Light

Poems of Spiritual Imagination

Stuart Higginbotham

A CROSSROAD BOOK

The Crossroad Publishing Company
www.crossroadpublishing.com

Copyright © 2024 by Stuart Higginbotham

All rights reserved. No part of this book may be reproduced, stored in a retrieval system, or transmitted, in any form or by any means, electronic, mechanical, photocopying, recording or otherwise, without the written permission of The Crossroad Publishing Copmpany, Printed in the United States of America

CIP Info:
Library of Congress Cataloging-in-Publication Data
Identifiers: LCCN 2024004830 | ISBN 9780824589042 (paperback)
Subjects: LCGFT: Poetry.
Classification: LCC PS3608.I363 B66 2024 | DDC 811/.6--dc23/eng/20240205
LC record available at https://lccn.loc.gov/2024004830

Welcome

These are poems of spiritual imagination, something we could claim as a virtue for our age when so much around us seems to grasp for a cold certainty tinged with fear. I began intensely writing poems in December 2019, at the start of the Advent season, oblivious to how the world would change a mere three months later. Throughout the deepest days of the pandemic and beyond, I kept writing and paying attention to the images that arose.

Looking back on the three years that gave rise to these poems, I am curious how we all struggled to imagine a new way forward. How do we see the world now? How are we still struggling to articulate how our lives have changed? How have we noticed the language and images that have become tattered? How have we explored new language and images to help us make sense of our souls?

When I laid these forty poems out on my dining room table, I saw the bodhisattva Tara speaking to the Greek tyrant Agamemnon. I saw my grandmother still offering wisdom and guidance from her seat in the Communion of Saints. I saw connections between the cobblestones of Parisian alleyways and the thick soil of the Mississippi Delta.

What is the common element? What makes these individual poems sing in harmony? For me, there is a hope to see how in even hesitant language we can nurture a yearning to imagine a way to be more human.

"Inside this pencil," the poet W. S. Merwin wrote, lies a collection of images and wonders that seek to flow out to help make sense of the depths of life. Each of us holds a pencil as we dare to pause, look within our hearts, and press the tip to the page.

Stuart

Stuart Higginbotham

Bones of Light

When the world is soaked in fear,
crashing storms throughout the night,
remember who we are
held up by bones of light.

A Hard-Won Wisdom

Come, Job, and sit with us by the fire.
Let us wipe your brow with a cool cloth.
And they whispered:
> An evil has happened to you.
> We saw, we watched from the top of our hill.

A fire danced within them while
I remembered:

> You will stand.
>> Who is this?
>> I am standing.
> You will answer.
>> Where were you?
>> I am speaking.

The chains that bound the Pleiades
now cut into my ankles.

Awe is to look down the tunnel of my own existence
and see the pupil of God's eye dilate with a fierceness.

In my eyes, dense as coal pressed into diamond,
they see a truth and they hold their breath,

for we worship a god who is not only sun
but eclipse as well.

A broken heart filled with love
spills onto the tile floor
when my wife makes tea.

I know what I said and
I know who I am.
I can still see the scar on my arm from the sore–
my own bitter stigmata.
I remember
and I rise to my feet before you
and we talk together in the cool of the evening breeze.

The Ghost of Agamemnon

The ghost of Agamemnon
keeps seducing us all, luring
with words dripping like honey that feed
the place within us that is starved
for something more, you see,
a drive, to feel intensity, to rally
against the day's foe,
to win at all cost, unleash woe
with an illusion of nobility
fed from the parched void
of his own soul's lack,
from the deep black crevice,
the hollowness.

He will say all this is
for a righteous purpose, even love,
but that is a most severe lie.

Narcissus Lives

He doesn't sit gently by pools anymore,
leaning over to watch
his own reflection looking back
at himself, caught up in his own gaze.
A thing of beauty, he thinks,
as he dips his finger into the water,
making ripples into waves,
sending minnows into a frenzy.

Now he sits upright
and looks around at every screen
that gladly shows the image
he has so willfully crafted—
and which so many so willingly purchase.

We each can either hold the mirror
in which he is reflected
or we can smash the glass
on the smooth stone of our own intention
to live a life cut free
of other people's shallow ambitions.

Fathom

I have seen on old maps,
with faded lines and frayed edges,
vast areas of empty space,
unknown and uncharted.

Ancient cartographers
sat with their hands in their laps
once they had written
all they knew and had seen.

One brave soul took up a quill,
looked into the void, and wrote
"Here there be dragons."
And there were–

at least in the fears
of those who craved to know more
and to grasp what they could imagine–
the ink fresh on the page.

And there in the depths,
iridescent scales reflected
the light of the sun as bodies heaved
and broke through the surface of the water.

What Soaks in the Fiber

We live in a time being written, that is forming still
out of the mists of our dreams, the shapes we fill

with wet ink on a clean, crisp page.
What soaks in the fiber will define our age.

When all around us fear rages with a screaming sound,
we crave control and wrestle oracles to the ground.

We stand with hesitant feet, clasped hands on the cusp,
and as for what the next step will bring, we can only trust

that we will at least lean toward healing and peace,
with enough love at our fingertips to soothe broken bodies.

May we reach out our arms toward another,
a stranger with whom we share the same Mother.

The Crimson Cord

May the pain of the world touch
my soul. It will not stay.
I cannot hold onto it,
but in a moment of contact, the power
of a storm in a raven's wing.

There is only one pain, shared
between all that breathes and lives,
the deep wisdom only whispered,
the key that unlocks all the ancient doors
whose hinges are stiff from fear.

Gently, gently pull the crimson cord
you hold between your fingers,
and it will lead you to the one
next to you, to the one you hate,
and to yourself.

Stuart Higginbotham

The Watchpost (Habakkuk's Mantle)

The oracle speaks.
Layers of whispers sound
like sand poured through fingers.
Prayer leaves a grit in my mouth.

There is an urge from somewhere,
and if I could only separate the grains,
line them up on a piece of dark paper,
a clearer picture would emerge:
> even a mere pause of
> violence, hatred,
> destruction, and greed.

How long will I cry out
and you will not answer?

I will stand at my watchpost.

Yet wisdom says that the rampart is not high
but deep within, that in the cave of my heart
the cliff rises where I can stand and see
the work that soothes the struggle,
> the work of my own soul,
> the awareness of your desire
> and my own resistance.

Bones of Light

Someone let loose a lie
that life would naturally improve,
that somehow goodness would gather speed
like water flowing downhill.

But wholeness is a buried gem,
excavated from a heart of stone.
Each blow of the hammer on the rock
inspires hope to sing in the veins:
      a desire to be free.

The entrance to the cave
is locked to all but me,
and the One who dreams me is already within
holding the key to open myself.

For there is still a vision.

My god

"My god," she says, as though
it was a plastic toy from the pile
heaped in the corner of her room,
marked off with yellow caution tape:
"No Trespassing."

But I have mine too, if I'm honest,
and I think mine would beat hers in a fight,
if they were matched up,
squaring off in the ring,
with the man holding a microphone
calling for everyone's attention.

When Agamemnon mustered the Greeks
to sail East to recapture his prize–
or so he told them–
only a slice from his blade
across his own daughter's pale neck
would convince the goddess
to let the winds fly free.

It turns out that having a god
tucked in your back pocket
may cost you a lot more
than you would like.

Footprints of the Angel of Mercy

We worship gods of wax and wood,
sculpted in our most clever moments,
biting our lips with focused eyes,
trying to capture a craving in solid form
with the force of our will and our fingers.

Beneath this urge to grasp,
there is a flame which cannot be held,
touching our lips for the briefest moment
with a kiss of grace.

At some point, the wax drips or dries
and the wood itself turns to dust
as the stone floor cradles our broken illusions.

The flecks of paint and chipped plaster
are the footprints of the angel of mercy.

I kneel once again in silence
with warmth on the palms of my hands,
the smell of frankincense,
the light on my face,
and the sound of music in my ears.

Incarnation

There are lines everywhere:
>hop-scotch chalk on a sidewalk with children
>skipping,
>steel walls anchored deep in the earth, fear gripping.

The impulse to set a boundary is ancient.
Motivation is always the question at hand.

Forgive us our trespasses
even as we secretly hope for you
to trespass against our cold clarity
(the deepest prayers are often whispered).

My skin is cracked from polishing my definitions.
I hope to preserve or defend
your dignity and power, I tell myself,
but it is most likely the care for my own
that pushes my pencil.

You, God, who lives next door, Rilke once wrote.
Waiting for a dinner invitation,
a gentle conversation,
or just a glance in the hallway when I recognize

myself in your eyes.
How long have you lived here?

While we mend fences,
you leap from immortality's edge
and plunge into the waters of my soul.

Let it be with me.
As your desire touches my willingness,
sparks fly. A line is crossed.
Can you possibly come among us
if some part of you is held back?
If some part of myself?

You want to taste my life?
Go ahead. It is your own.

The shortest distance between two points
is a straight line,
unless there is only one point.

Stuart Higginbotham

Strike a Match

I woke up last Thursday
and my entire image of God
had changed, not all at once,
but completely.

God, the word, is a piece of slick paper
my soul cannot grip any longer.

God had always been something–Someone–
I prayed to, but now, somehow,
God was something–somewhere, even–
I pray from.

Such a deep awareness
empties me out of whatever
had filled me in the moment
just before this one.

Now, I sit quietly as the birds
sing the day into life.
Water pours through cupped hands, and
what is kept open can be filled–

emptied of what
and filled with what?

These are the questions I carry gently,
fragile creatures I could crush
in one thoughtless moment of grasping.

Take the prayer card out of your pocket,
strike a match, and light it on fire.
Watch the flame dance.
Only then does it become truly alive.

Stuart Higginbotham

Truth Lit From Behind

We so quickly claim that our time,
this day, this moment,
is full of more struggle than others,
the times of those who are now
ghosts and memory.

Never before, they say.
No one has ever.
Unprecedented.

The bow slides sharply across the string,
and the note soars past what our ears can hear,
but we feel the pressure of
skin pulled tight against a bone
in this time that is our own.

My grandfather was shot five times
in the war, left for dead
on the cold Italian dirt while others sang carols
in candle-lit churches.
His young widow grieved at home
until news came days later—
but what of those tears she had shed?

Bones of Light

When he was an old man,
my wife once saw an X-ray of his chest,
the shape of his heart there on the wall,
the truth lit from behind
with the thin lines of metal dust
streaking across his torso,
five paths to follow
from youth to adulthood with eyes
open to life, stretched so wide.

Threads strain to hold
the patterns we crave to sew together.
Jesus said something
about new wine in old wineskins,
and I need to read that again.

We don't see life as it is,
we see life as we are.
The wise have always known this
to be true, with our call to cleanse
the lens of our own sight,
to gently polish the glass
on which we press our faces,
looking, always searching.

My eye rests on the flower made of flame
that stands tall among the stones
as I take my next step,
as will those who follow after.

Transfiguration

It is not change we fear
but growth, because to open
our hearts to such potential,
a wide field beyond the wall,
demands that we each hope.

When Moses came down from the mountain
he put a veil on his face.

What we can be we are not now,
and what we are now
does not bind us–
the shackles of our present pain disintegrating.

For now we see in a mirror dimly.

There is within us a light.
Within we are light.
Deeply beats the steady pulse
that transfigures, beginning
in our hard bones and
seeping outward through tissues
to our skin, a holy sweat
glistening in the morning sun.

The life was the light of all people.

Stay close to Hafez
with the light of our own being
and we may yet be saved.

Magic

Magic is very real.
It is just not what they taught us it was–
like love.

Love is very real
but looks nothing like it did when I was a child–
tastes nothing like it did either.

Only when I saw our daughter
being born of water and blood
did I even begin to understand

I had much to learn.
Only when I whispered "Thank you"
in my peaceful grandmother's ear,

her body still warm,
did I even catch a glimpse of
the deepest truth in all things.

The Gift of Tears

I want to stretch out
the arms of my soul
and cradle the brokenness
of my own life.

I will find you there.

Who first said that
to be strong means to hold it together,
even in spaces drenched with tears
or unspeakable fears?
And when did we first believe this lie?

To bear it, composed,
all of this, with a strained face pulled tight,
to bottle up the force of life,
which leaves a mark most severe and deep–

whose hands have such strength
and who dares to try, and is it not heresy?

Stuart Higginbotham

To be well, we must truly be and
that may be the bravest thing of all.

Let me pick up Elijah's cloak
which he dropped in the mouth of the cave,
stunned into silence at a presence most piercing.
Let me wrap it around my body and feel
the memory of warmth cut through
the dull cold of my sadness.

Can it not be that strength means
the courage to feel honestly and fully
turn toward my neighbor and let
the truth of my own being
flow out of my soul,
with the energy of that gentle touch
between us suddenly lighting
the cave of my heart like a thousand suns?

I will find you there.

We stack the wounds of our life like a cairn
and then tread lightly lest it crumble around us
when feet fall too heavily.
We place a hand over the mouth of the pain
we need to share and choke off
what may be most human–
what might save us all.

Bones of Light

The gift of tears is the sacred fruit
of a living soul, a flame in the dark
we can kiss with a gentle breath
and protect with cradled hands,
the light that yearns to nurture
the seed of compassion with the warmth
of a union most holy.

Our tears are a holy water
too precious to keep in a marble font.

The Muses

Let me tell you a secret
that has changed my life
and carried me beyond and through
moments of fear into a place of trust,
a henge of stone with oaks,
their branches shielding my soul
in the hottest part of the day.

They are real, the muses,
that is only one thing to call them.
They have many names,
as do you and I, spaciousness and
light wrapped in skin.

I saw one once in a coffee cup,
but it wasn't long before it flashed
and flew outside to dance with
the goldfinch on the purple coneflower.

Mine is quite fond of the dawn,
those first moments when my eyes open
and I eavesdrop on the birds outside.

Bones of Light

Some prefer fists raised high, first breaths
or last, an unresolved chord,
the brush of lips, water over rock.

Don't press them too hard for a name,
because they can see through
your urge to control, and they'll play with you–
just ask Moses about the bush–
not the answer he wanted.

At best we stitch a net within our souls
made from hope and desire,
the holy threads that connect us
to our deepest selves, where
they take our hands and whisper
fresh words that inspire
as we wait patiently and trust–
which is the most sublime practice of all.

With Life

But what of the deep force within, a fierce yearning with life,
the pulse in the heart of a creature, burning with life.

The wind blows across the sea with a salt spray so strong,
tears flow like a memory returning with life.

I once read that it is next Spring's fresh bud that pushes
the red leaf from the branch, seasons turning with life.

Each soul is given the space to grow in wisdom,
not merely to gain knowledge but to savor learning with life.

Now the poet sits by the fire at the end of a cold day
with gratitude for any fruit of black ink he may be earning
with life.

Illumination

But of the light we cannot speak
fully, but we must try
to open our mouths and wait
for some word to fall short–
yet even that reach is rooted in You.

I once saw my grandmother
held by the sunlight, standing
between two sheets while hanging clothes
on a warm morning–
an illumination, with her silhouette
a faint shadow and a thing of beauty
when she raised her arms as if to dance.

Stuart Higginbotham

The Oracle

I cast the hosts on the wooden table
and gather them gently in my hands

looking for the writing with my eyes–
the other ones–
the word of the One from whom
no secrets are hid.

The questions which have no answers
must still be asked.

In the asking itself we are
most wonderfully human,
wrestling with divinity once again.

We yearn to stand at an angle
to see the light shine through,
and all is connected and we remember again
the message we have always been told.

A Manifestation of Sapphire

It is believed
our ancestors could not see the color blue.

Homer spoke of a wine-red Aegean.
Now Vishnu's body dances across the universe as
Our Lady pulls her mantle across her shoulder.

The structure of the eye
needed to develop,
a space in the heart to imagine
beyond an unknown horizon.

The miracle of a hummingbird wing.
The depth of a violet.
The truth of a thistle.

The color blue waited on them
to become ready, until the moment
when a young girl lifted her eyes
to the sky and beheld a manifestation of sapphire,
seeing that for which she had no reference.

What did she tell her mother?

Tara

Out of the rock she rises
greeting the seeker bent low,
threadbare hope in hand.

Her right leg stretched out,
a perpetual intention of love,
arms in a posture of praise.

A figure in stone with more life
than a thousand of flesh and blood,
stillness pulsing with a finger's kiss.

The teacher told us
even the rocks would cry out,
so why are we surprised?

I long to feel the impulse
of love pushing through
the hardness in my own soul.

The Healing of all Things

Hope indeed lands on your tongue
in that place where lemons flirt
with warm honey,
both of these full of the memory
of sharpness and sweet consolation,
standing side by side and whispering to you
of the healing of all things.

Stuart Higginbotham

For Holy Saturday

The boatman, with a keen eye, lays down his oar,
watching the man walk slowly toward the far shore

of this river dark as ink, a place betwixt
life and death, his wounded feet blessing the Styx.

No coins were offered to enter this ancient hell,
but three drops of blood from his hand fell

and mingled with the water, itself now set free,
while hand in hand they walked into eternity.

Toward the Breaking Dawn

You will speak to me of woe
and I, too, will speak to you of what I know
of stones rolled away from tombs
and graves cracked open with
hands reaching toward the breaking dawn,
as rivers flow once more on parched beds,
carving channels into dry desert rock
now singing with life again.

Hermetic

You, wisp of fine white smoke,
kiss of the breeze on my lips,
smooth as silk that slips
through the tight crack
in well-crafted plans.

Like oil flowing through a stack of dry stones,
the boundary I set firmly,
between what is mine and yours
is transgressed.

"Come here," you say, softly,
beyond the best that thoughts can be,
with the mind always seeking to frame the question,
name the mystery and
claim it with a clenched fist.

Thick clouds above us and a rumble of thunder,
then life's truth sweeps through the trees:
this moment, then transformed
into a fresh thing.

Bones of Light

I stand at the edge of the river,
clear as glass and steadily flowing
as I reach for your hand.

When an Elder Dies

For Don

We sit by your bedside
listening for the sound of breath.
Softly now, the gentle rise
of the white blanket across your chest,
your heartbeat drawing closer in this noble silence.

A sage once said when an elder dies
a library burns,
the holy flame kissing the knowledge once held firm
as it transforms, tight threads now loosened.
All held so firmly is now released,
set free, rising like the finest ash
into a night filled with stars.

Your wisdom now diffuses,
frankincense on the hot coal of divine love,
a pungent sweetness
filling the room, a perfume of memory.

From the moment you walked
amongst the trees and felt

Bones of Light

that which cannot be named—but must—
you lived your life.
You were not perfect; you were true.

The best ones of us are always blind
to their own brightness
while we warm our cold hands,
sitting close to their wondering souls.

Now, the sheet that covers your body
unfurls, tight with the wind
which carried you into this world
and which now lifts your soul to the shores
you have so longed for—
that you remembered,
that waited for you.

Stuart Higginbotham

Tradition and Taxidermy

My bicycle leans against the wooden post
with the red and white pole spinning.
Inside the glass door, the old magazines
wait there on the table.

I step into the room,
a chapel in its own way,
filled with relics of sylvan crusades,
a surreal anamnesis on the wall.

Tufted fur and feathers are splayed,
interspersed with the plastic sheen of
scales and still fins and faded plaques,
a silent chorus with glass marble eyes
all chanting a macabre cantata of bygone glory.

Faded vestments with patches worn smooth,
balding spots and sun-bleached turkey wattle.
Each liturgy opens with the exchange:
"Did I tell you about the time?"
"I don't think you did."

Bones of Light

The music begins with the solid hum
of clippers like deep-throated monks calling us to prayer.
There is a notable absence of confession.
For Communion, their memories are placed in my hands.

The sweet spirit of nostalgia
is soaked into the curtains like tobacco smoke.

In my imagination, I take the glass jar
of antiseptic water by the mirror,
asperge the choir with a plastic comb,
and watch as they come alive and sing,
waking to freedom once again.

Stuart Higginbotham

Only Now

When the unforeseen
steps into my frame of perception,
a choice is offered.

A falcon flies near,
landing in front of me on the branch
as I sit on my hill
sipping black and rose tea,
trying to focus on my breath.

The unexpected grace of pure awareness
on silent wings,
an angel of death and beauty,
only now, in this moment.

Machado's Dream

He walks alone deep into the night
on pine-lined trails with scattered rock,
pupils full with only the moon's light.
Cries of pain in the valley below.
A tired body dragging memories uphill.

His worn hands hold the leather case
filled with sheets of paper, ink and dreams,
incantations safely gathered
with a prayer for a time more human.

Hope pulls him forward into the green,
bushes grasping his legs as he steps through.
And there a cave, the sanctuary of Pan,
the wild one who knows freedom,
and a moment of breath with a chorus of cicadas.

The thought comes swiftly of hidden poems.
Let the womb hold them safely away from death,
to come again with fairer skies,
birdsong rather than bullets.

But he never returned.

Last night the rusted latch broke open,
cracked with time as a strong wind
lifted the cover and set the worn pages free,
a flock of sparrows scattering in the night.

Making a Mark

His fingers are stained
with the perfect mixture
of charcoal and cigarette smoke.

"Time does not pass on your face,"
he says simply to the man,
as if they had known one another forever.

He strikes with absolute conviction,
making the first black mark
on the crisp white paper.

The Tomb of St. Genevieve

The worn glass case with brass moldings,
a carved lid the length of a body
once held inside before they burned the bones.

Folded paper holding the prayers of pilgrims,
some nestled on the stone
whispering softly still while I stand unblinking.

In this chapel, a pope once knelt
giving thanks for a young life
where candles now dance in the shadows.

The Things That Are Sown

My grandmother grew roses
in the hot Arkansas sun,
with my eyes fixed on her
walking through her garden
with ranks of pine trees
towering like rooted columns
in our private cathedral that was
censed with sweet, dripping resin
and a carpet of St. Augustine grass
pushing between my toes.

Put off thy shoes from thy feet.

Our procession continued
with her dropping seeds that
took root and spread life,
beauty rising in her wake.

And as the garden causeth
the things that are sown in it
to spring forth.

Her sheets with faded flowers
flew like prayer flags, catching the wind
and announcing to all that we are loved.

My First Spell

I once walked with my grandfather
next to twelve rows of tall, sweet corn,
a choir robed in green,
hands raised in praise of the sun,
with roots holding the hot dirt like long toes.

Dark clouds came closer, over my shoulder.
Thunder rumbled, silencing the birds.
He lifted the axe he held at his side
and sliced the air above his head

while blowing as hard as he could—
all this while I watched,
learning the spell and wondering if
it would protect against the coming storm.

Stuart Higginbotham

An Exercise in Release

I keep a small stack of poems
tucked in the pocket of my blue jacket
next to peppermint,

printed on white paper
with only my name
written at the bottom of each one.

I keep them close at hand,
the penciled prayers, within reach
for when I hear that voice, gently leading,

and then I hide them,
leaving each one in a place
where they may be found–or not.

I hid one at the grocery store,
behind cans of cream of mushroom soup,
surely to be discovered quickly.

Another was slipped between packets
of Echinacea seeds, with hopes
to take bloom in later Spring.

Then there was the one placed in a collection
of T. S. Eliot poems at the library–
that one was an offering.

A waitress at the Mexican restaurant named
"The Pineapple" found one on a Thursday
in March with bright blue skies.

There is one that is hidden away,
not meant to be seen by any eyes,
resting beneath a stone on a favorite trail.

It is an exercise in release,
a way to practice a lesson so difficult for me:
trusting that things can find their way.

Stuart Higginbotham

For the Trees

On that day, the clouds
a pale gray blanket
tucking me close to the earth,
I will slowly lift my eyes and
see you standing tall, your leaves
like green pearls gently draped
across your neck, and I will
keep silent and understand
that the trees have always known.

Everywhere

If you dig down
deep enough in one place,
you'll come out everywhere.

As This Dance Unfolds

"It is no longer I who live,"

Is He becoming me,
or am I becoming Him?

No matter which it is,
neither of us will be the same
as this dance unfolds.

All There is

There is

>   within me
>   within you

>   within all

>   Light.

>   At the end
>   in the beginning

>   it will be

all there is.

Stuart Higginbotham

The Shaman Sits by the Fire (A Love Letter to Clergy)

The shaman's tent sits outside the wall
or at least at the edge,
a vision to be gained by one,
a place to be reached by others
who seek a truth in all things,
beneath and within.

There I sit.
Is it not a space of lonely union?

To be set aside is to be placed
within, a mystery, not just another–
as if there is an other to see or be.

Nothing less than a soul I yearn to be,
driven to become one, aware,
drawn into and through my own life,
swallowed through the center of my own being
and finding you resting there.

Bones of Light

How can we dare speak of it?

I hold a beaten bronze bowl,
smooth to my finger's touch.
I stretch out my hand
and gather prayers like blown glass,
gently placing them inside,
for that is the only place that
the burning truth of them will not singe.

As I slowly peer over the rim,
my eyes rest on what lies there,
catching but a glimpse of
the clearness of things, the more
that is here but not seen
and the wound of ignorance that I carry.

In quiet moments when the wind brushes by,
the prayers spoken long ago
reach out their hands through time.
How could I have known
that which is my soul, and yours?

While the world shouts around me,
Orpheus whispers in my ear
with a fierce truth, a vision drawn near
of that space where love and grief join hands.
The hope of imagined things.
Do not look back.
Do not look back.

Stuart Higginbotham

Yes, my soul knows well the one
who crosses the veil on winged feet,
silent and swift and full of focus,
the one known by all who step through
and visit the unknown–and back again.
The one who takes the hand and guides
those whose time has come.

The shaman fans the coals
with life still in them.
All would do well to remember
deep down and hold close to
the burning flame that lies
at the heart of who they are,
the holy burden of what they can be–
and must.

About the Author

The Rev. **Stuart Higginbotham**, DMin, joined the Candler faculty in 2023. His work focuses especially on contextual education within the Episcopal and Anglican Studies program. He was ordained an Episcopal priest in 2008 and has served as the rector of Grace Episcopal Church in Gainesville, Georgia, since 2014. He has served in many leadership roles within the Episcopal Diocese of Atlanta and has also led retreats and workshops throughout the United States.

Higginbotham's vocation focuses on the connections between the wisdom of the ancient Christian contemplative tradition and the current dynamics of congregational ministry. Both his pastoral and academic work draw on Christian and interfaith sources to nurture faithful and sustainable embodiments of ministry. He is the author of *The Heart of a Calling: The Practice of Christian Mindfulness in Congregational Ministry* (Crossroad, 2021) and is co-editor of *Contemplation and Communion: A Gathering of Fresh Voices for a Living Tradition (Crossroad, 2019)*, as well as other articles and contributions.

About The Publisher

Since 1798, under respected imprints including Crossroad Books and Herder & Herder, we have published to the fundamental questions all humans ask: Where do I come from? Why am I here? Where am I going? Rooted in the Judeo-Christian tradition we promote writing and reading as time-tested disciplines for focus, discourse and expansion of consciousness. Our books travel the world connecting people, telling stories, arguing ideas and aiming to amplify beneficial spiritual energy in prayer and contemplation. Our expertise and passion is to provide wholesome spiritual nourishment. We sit on a treasure chest of wisdom forged through the ages and want to help make sure that what is relevant we, the human family, take into this new just beginning age.

www.ingramcontent.com/pod-product-compliance
Lightning Source LLC
LaVergne TN
LVHW042055070225
803225LV00038B/825